A Day in My Town

David Blanche

INFOMAX COMMON CORE READERS

Rosen Classroom™

New York

Published in 2013 by The Rosen Publishing Group, Inc.
29 East 21st Street, New York, NY 10010

Book Design: Michael Harmon

Photo Credits: Cover Peter Pearson/Stone/Getty Images; p. 4 Chris Rogers/Photolibrary/Getty Images; p. 5 Panoramic Images/Panoramic Images/Getty Images; pp. 6, 15 Mat Hayward/Shutterstock.com; pp. 7, 15 © iStockphoto.com/kirin_photo; pp. 8, 15 Mike Harrington/Digital Vision/Getty Images; pp. 9, 10 David Hanover/Stone/Getty Images; pp. 10, 15 Meridian Studios/The Image Bank/Getty Images; pp. 11, 15 © iStockphoto.com/kali9; p. 12 Smith Collection/Iconica/Getty Images; p. 13 Lasrs Klove Photo Service/Riser/Getty Images; p. 14 Jeff Greenberg/Photolibrary/Getty Images; p. 15 Chris Stein/Lifesize/Getty Images

ISBN: 978-1-4488-8977-8
6-pack ISBN: 978-1-4488-8978-5

Manufactured in the United States of America

CPSIA Compliance Information: Batch #WS12RC: For further information contact Rosen Publishing, New York, New York at 1-800-237-9932.

Word Count: 126

Contents

Saturday is a busy day in my town.

Everyone has something to do.

Many people live in my neighborhood.
I see people doing many things.

I ride my bike to visit my friends.

We play with our toys.

We have lots of fun!

Mrs. Gold works at her store.

She sells flowers.

I buy flowers from her.

I give the flowers to my mom.
They make her very happy!

Mr. Butler likes to drive his car.

He keeps it very clean.

Jenny and Kate play with their dog.

Their dog is so cute!

My sister likes to dance.

She dances to her music.

I have a dog.

Her name is Mittens.

I take her for a walk.

What do you like to do in your town?

My Busy Town

Words to Know

bike

neighborhood

store

Index